The Treasure Book
of Chinese Martial Arts

The Treasure Book of Chinese Martial Arts

Dynamic of Power Generation
(Volume 2)

Peter Jaw

Copyright © 2007 by Peter Jaw.

ISBN: Hardcover   978-1-4257-8591-8
          Softcover   978-1-4257-8571-0

All rights reserved. No part of this book may be reproduced or transmitted in any form or by any means, electronic or mechanical, including photocopying, recording, or by any information storage and retrieval system, without permission in writing from the copyright owner.

This book was printed in the United States of America.

To order additional copies of this book, contact:
Xlibris Corporation
1-888-795-4274
www.Xlibris.com
Orders@Xlibris.com
42315

CONTENTS

Foreword 7

Part I: Elements of Power

Chapter 1:   Directional Factor 11
Chapter 2:   Source of Power 18
Chapter 3:   Emptiness and Fullness 21
Chapter 4:   Flow 23
Chapter 5:   Understanding the Opponent's Power 26
Chapter 6:   Interaction 28

Part II: Characteristic Power

Chapter 7:   Xing Yi 33
Chapter 8:   Tai Chi 35
Chapter 9:   Ba Gua 38
Chapter 10: Ba Ji 43
Chapter 11: Tong Bei 46

Part III: Development of Power

Chapter 12: Relaxation Exercise 51
Chapter 13: Standing Practice 52
Chapter 14: Equipment Training 55
Chapter 15: Partner Training 58

Concluding Remark 61

Foreword

In the previous book "The Treasure Book of Chinese Martial Arts (volume 1)", how to analyze a technique and how to study Chinese martial arts with 3 golden methods: analysis, practice and technique are examined. In the current book, how to study and practice power (Jin) generation is discussed.

If we do not understand the generation, flow and interaction of a power from our moves and postures, then we are doing wasted moves. Our study and practice are in vain and useless. In the beginning of study and practice, we may be asked to do or mimic moves and postures that we do not know anything about. However, once we familiarize ourselves with some basic moves and postures. The study and practice of power generation then become the next necessary step.

There are three parts in this book. The Part I elucidates the basic elements of a power. Specific kinds of power from 5 styles (Xing Yi, Tai Chi, Ba Gua, Ba Ji and Tong Bei) are explained in Part II. Finally, how to practice and develop these powers are discussed in Part III.

The basic elements of a power include directional factors (Chapter 1), source of power generation (Chapter 2), theory about emptiness and fullness (Chapter 3), flow of your power (Chapter 4), understanding the opponent's power (Chapter 5), and interaction of your power with that of the opponent (Chapter 6).

The basic characteristic powers from 5 styles are discussed as examples in Part II. If you study these 5 styles, the information will be very important to know. If you study styles other than those five, the information will be good to study as examples to help you understand your own particular style. These 5 styles are also discussed in the previous volume. The reader may refer to both volumes and have an overall understanding of the styles, how everything works, why and how we do the moves/postures the way we are asked to.

Finally, how to do relaxation exercise, how to do standing practice to develop static and tensile strength, how to use equipments to develop power generation, and how to train with partners to understand power flow and interaction are discussed in Part III.

The actual fighting techniques are used as examples throughout the text. The reader may relate the discussion of theory with actual practice together. Review questions are provided at the end of each chapter. They are designed to refresh the reader's understanding of the content.

This book is a must read for students practicing some style of martial arts. This book is also a good reference source for readers that like to understand how moves and postures work in general for the purpose of fighting.

Lastly, this book is written in the context of hand to hand combat. The anatomy and physics are only mentioned within the context or usage of open hand fighting. For human anatomy, physiology, and physics, readers may refer to medical books and professionals. This book is for information only. For actual practice of martial arts, please consult your martial arts teacher.

Laguna Beach

Peter Jaw

Part I

Elements of Power

To understand the nature of a power, at first, we may characterize it according to the direction it travels (Chapter 1). Secondly, we have to know how the power is generated from different parts of the body (Chapter 2). There is a theory of emptiness and fullness in terms of a power flowing from one side of the body toward the limbs (Chapter 3). How to transfer the power from one side of the body to another side efficiently is in Chapter 4. How to test and listen to the power from the opponent is in Chapter 5. How to use a small power to interact with opponent's bigger power and defeat him is in Chapter 6.

Chapter 1

Directional Factor

I. Definition of Li and Jin:

In physics, the force is equal to the mass timed by acceleration or F=MA. In Chinese, the force is described as Li. On the other hand, Jin means the strength or kinetic energy that is generated. For the purpose of discussion in this book, we use "power" to mean Jin.

II. The traveling path:

The power may travel from the source and move forward, backward, upward, downward, circularly and laterally. We use our muscle, tendon, bone and joints to produce power, we then transfer that power to our hand, foot, elbow, knee, shoulder and hip etc. Due to gravity from the earth, when we produce a power to move toward a defined direction, there is also a counter power generated by our body to balance our posture.

III. The interaction:

When we contact with the opponent, the power we produced is then transferred or relayed onto the opponent via the contact points. We may deliver a focused power to injure soft spots and internal organs of the opponent. We may also deliver power in different points to uproot the balance and throw the opponent from his position.

IV. Categorization of a power by its direction:

1. Forward trusting power (Chong Jin)

How to produce a forward power:

You place your fist (Chui) around your waist and then you suddenly punch forward or thrust forward your fist (Chong Chui). We may rotate the waist or move forward with the steps at the same time to generate more power by recruiting the rotation of the waist or whole body movement. The closer you are to target area, more power and damage is delivered.

A wide power:

You may also punch your vertical fist forward with a bent elbow along your center line. This is also called a "character sun" fist. Your fist is flat vertically just like the Chinese character for sun. If you use a horizontal fist, it is called Ping Quan. Both have wide area of contact.

A pointed power:

If you protrude the knuckle of the index finger, this is called a "eagle beak" fist. If you protrude the middle finger's knuckle, it is called a "penetrating bone" fist. These are for focused point contact at soft spots, pressure points along the midline of the body or the heart etc.

Alignment of joints:

If you are using Chui or Ping Quan, the wrist joint has to be straight. If you use focused knuckle fist, we have to align or angle the wrist joint. So that we protect the wrist joint and relay the counterforce upon contact all the way to the shoulder joint and the rest of the body.

The main point is that either the knuckle or the face of the fist has to be straight or aligned with the wrist, the elbow and the shoulder for the power to be going evenly forward and at the same time, receive the counterforce evenly backward.

2. Retreating power (Che Jin)

When you retract your punching fist, you may open your palm and grab the opponent's blocking hand back. At the same time, you punch forward with your other hand. The punching forward power is balanced by your pulling hand back or Luo Shou.

When you retract your punching fist, you focus on your elbow moving back. When you punch forward, your rib side is also open. If the opponent is attacking your open rib side, your elbow moving back will move away the attack.

If you are doing a "long fist" style, you may move your hand all the way back to your waist line. If you are doing a close quarter (short range) combat, you may move your hand back to be near the elbow of the other hand so as to protect the elbow joint of the other hand.

If you kick backward, you may want to lean your upper body forward so as to balance your body. In practice, you may also punch forward the hand of the supporting leg while kick back the other foot. Again, we have to balance our power flow from the left to the right or from trusting forward and retreating backward.

3. Upward lifting power (Tuo Jin)

We may use our palm to lift the opponent's elbow. The power is expressed in the center of the palm.

Upward pushing power (Ding Jin)

We may move our fist upward to hit the opponent's groin, abdomen, chest and chin etc. If you move your fist upward and forward at the same time, it is called an extending fist or Cheng Chui.

Upward and lateral power (Tiao Jin)

If you move your forearm upward to deflect the opponent's wrist and forearm upward an laterally, it is called Tiao. It is a common defense move for head, neck and upper body area.

Upward spiral power (Zuan Jin)

When you spiral your hand/palm upward as if a small hawk soaring upward, it is called drilling palm or Zuan Zhang (Ba Gua). At first, you rotate your forearm inward or counterclockwise, and then you rotate your forearm outward or clockwise.

You may also drill your closed fist forward; it is then called Zuan Quan (Xing Yi).

4.   Downward pressing power (An Jin)

We may push our palm downward at the opponent's abdomen. We also bend our knees and lower our hips as if sitting downward. Our palm has more power from the whole body going downward at the same time. This is called sinking palm or Xia Cheng Zhang (Ba Gua).

When we do downward palm with both hands, it is called the bear stance. Not only the palms but also the whole body is moving or sinking downward.

5.   Circular power (Chan Jin)

Silk reeling (Chan Si)

There can be circular movements from all joints. If we rotate around the wrist, elbow and shoulder joint, it is called Chan Wan, Chan Zhou, and Chan Bei. The circling around the wrist joint is also called small entanglement or Xiao Chan. The circling around the shoulder joints, it is called big entanglement of Da Chan.

Cloud hand (Yun Shou):

When we move our forearm inward or clockwise around the elbow joint. We turn over our palm as if folding a towel. We then continue to draw our hand outward. This is called "waving the cloud" or Yun Shou. We complete drawing a circle in front of our vital area of the chest and abdomen.

Use of Chan Si:

The circular movements are used to contact and deflect the opponent's wrist and forearm as defensive moves. We may also restrain the opponent's arm and open his vital area. We may also use them for attack or throw the opponent.

6.   Lateral power (Heng Jin)

The first 4 directions are considered as a linear power or Zhi Jin. If we approach them horizontally, it is called a horizontal power or Heng Jin. It can travel either to the left, right, upward or downward.

Interrupting power (Lie Jin)

By introducing a horizontal power, we may interrupt the opponent's linear power. It is also called Lie.

Intercepting power (Lan Jin)

If we follow the direction of the opponent's linear power for the most part and only introduce a little force laterally, it is then called intercept or Lan. It may also be called Gua.

Confining power (Gua Jin)

When you rotate your forearm and wrist from inward outward to press downward and laterally the opponent's wrist and forearm, it is also called Gua. This is also part of the cloud hand or Yun Shou. We do it from the inside of the opponent's arm.

These are examples of using a Heng Jin to neutralize a Zhi Jin.

Using a Zhi Jin to neutralize a Heng Jin:

If the opponent swings his fist horizontally to hit your temple, it is a Heng Jin. We may raise our forearm to Gua or Tiao. At the same time, we may punch forward with our other hand at his open chest and abdomen. This is called using Zhi Jin to neutralize Heng Jin.

How do we use the categorization above to analyze moves and postures?

At first, we categorize the move according to its directions. Secondly, we identify which part is defensive and which part is counterattack. Sometimes, a move may have both defensive and offensive purpose built in. Finally, we would conclude the move is to strike (Da), grapple (Qin Na) or throw (Shuai).

7. Position power (Zhou Jin)

It is not a real power per se. It is used to describe the power you would give up or gain from walking or stepping into a new position. It is very important to factor the position relative to your opponent in your evaluation of the overall power structure and interaction.

Moving in steps forward, backward, sideways, up and down are very important maneuvers. If the opponent moves forward toward us, we move backward or to the side. We create a power "gain" from stepping away. It is called walking power or Zhou Jin. If we do not move away, we need the "gained" or extra power to do a similar defense result.

Advantage of Zhou Jin:

This would constitute most of the advantage to neutralize the opponent's power. We may use a minimal power from a better position to deal with the opponent's power. This is a primary consideration for all moves and postures. We may not be stronger than the opponent, but we may outmaneuver him by stepping into the right direction which is away from the harm. At the same time, we may use our forearm to distance the opponent's forearm or legs from getting into our vital area of the chest, and abdomen.

Review:

1. What is the most important power?
2. What is "walking power"?
3. What are 4 general directions of a linear power?
4. How do we balance a forward traveling power?
5. Why is it important to align the fist, the wrist, the elbow and the shoulder, when we do a punch?
6. Is it a good idea to use our hand as a defensive move, when we move back the punching fist or pushing palm?
7. If we are not careful, we may hurt our wrist with a pushing at the root of the palm?
8. What is the purpose of a focused knuckle protruding fist?
9. Do we need a power traveling forward to balance our backward move?
10. What is the difference between a thrusting fist (Chong Chui) and an extending fist (Cheng Chui)?
11. What is Tiao?
12. What is a drilling fist or palm (Zuan)?
13. What is a sinking palm or Xia Cheng Zhang?
14. Do we have to lower our body with a sinking palm?
15. What is a bear stance?

16. Is a circular move around the wrist or Chan Wan a common defensive move?
17. What is a cloud hand or Yun Shou?
18. What is a common way of restraining and opening the opponent's door?
19. What directions are considered a linear power?
20. What are directions for a horizontal power?
21. How do you use a horizontal power to neutralize a linear power?
22. How do you use a linear power to neutralize a horizontal power?
23. What is Lie?
24. What is Lan?
25. What is Gua?
26. How would you analyze moves and postures with the directional factor of a power?

Chapter 2

Source of Power

The source:

The source of power is theorized to be from the flow of Qi. And Qi is stored in the center of gravity or elixirs field (Dan Tian) of the body. Due to the gravity from the earth, when we move and step on the ground, a counter energy is produced. We transfer the energy to our other body parts or limbs and deliver the energy into expression of a power. Thus, the root or source of power is from the feet.

The expression points:

The power may be expressed from the fist, the elbow and the shoulder of the upper limbs. The power may be expressed from the chest, the back and the waist of the body. The power may also be expressed from the hip, the knee and the foot of the lower limbs.

Ways of expression:

We may punch the fist (Chui) forward or swing the fist horizontally, upward or downward. The elbow (Zhou) may be advanced forward, horizontally, upward or downward. The shoulder joint may be used to contact the opponent first then strike outward with advancing steps. This is called Kao.

Traveling distance:

The power is generated from movements of muscle groups and rotation around the joints. The traveling distance would be from flexion to extension of joints. For example, the fist is near the waist line with a bent elbow. When you extend the elbow joint and move your fist forward, you also rotate upward your shoulder joint. The fist would travel no further than that with your fully extended elbow joint or the whole arm length. If you turn your upper body by rotating the waist, you may move your fist further. That is the arm length plus the body length from the midline of the body assuming you do not move your steps. If a fist travels a short distance, it is called a short power. If the fist only moves about an inch, it is called an inch power or Cun Jin. If the fist is traveling a long distance and continuing, it is considered a long power or Chang Jin.

Moving or stepping power (Zhou Jin)

The power may also come from moving steps forward. This is the movement of the whole body. It is from stepping or walking and called Zhou Jin. If a power comes from a whole body movement from the original starting position by moving steps, it is considered a complete body power or Zhen Jin.

Powers from the forearm:

The rotation of the forearm or Gun Zhou is also used to defend or attack. If you rotate the forearm inward, it is called wrapping or Guo. If you then rotate outward the forearm, it is called extending or Peng. If you bring both forearms close together, it is a closing posture or He. The power is called closing power or He Jin. If you then move both forearms outward and separate them, it is called opening posture or Kai. The power is called opening power or Kai Jin.

Review:

1. What are 3 power expression points of the upper limb?
2. What are 3 power expression areas of the body?
3. What are 3 power expression points of the lower limb?
4. What is Kao?
5. What is a Cun Jin?
6. What is a Chang Jin?
7. What is a walking power or Zhou Jin?
8. What is a complete power or Zhen Jin?
9. What is a wrapping power or Guo Jin?

10. What is an extending power or Peng Jin?
11. What is a closing power or He Jin?
12. What is an opening power or Kai Jin?
13. The power from the rotation of the forearm may be used to defend and attack?
14. Where is the source of power in the body?
15. How is a power generated? Via the flow of Qi?
16. Is a short power means an expression point travels only a short distance before reaching the end contact point?
17. What is an inch power or Cun Jin?
18. What is considered as a long power or Chang Jin?

Chapter 3

Emptiness and Fullness

A theory:

The emptiness and fullness of the power are used to describe the location in reference to distribution and expression of the power in the body. The two opposing terms are also used to describe the flow of the power in terms of progression of time.

If I move my right fist forward to punch, then my right fist is the full hand, i.e. the hand that has the full power. In contrast, my retracting left hand is the empty one. If I also rotate my waist with the right side forward, then the power is full on my right side of the body. My left side is moving toward the rear and away from the opponent, it is the empty side.

Progression of a power:

The power is lost or gone, once I reach the end of an extension or moving forward. The power may be transferred to the opponent via a contact point. Otherwise, my body absorbs all the power via stoppage or retention within the joints. The joints are considered as the stop points or retention points of a power. This is because the joints connecting the limbs pull and stop the advancement of your fist.

If I now switch to move my left fist forward while retracting my extended right fist, my left fist is the full hand and my right hand is the empty one. Once extended, the arm has to be retracted and bent before we may move it forward again.

If you use the same hand to punch forward, retract and punch forward again, then the same hand is the full and the empty hand alternately in time.

How to harness a power:

When we are getting into a preparation posture before we punch forward, it is called storing or harnessing the power (Xu Jin). Once we are in position, we then punch forward. This is called releasing, emitting or issuing the power (Fa Jin). For example, my right fist is pulling back, it is a process of storing power. When I punch forward with the right fist, it is called releasing the stored power or Fa Jin. When we reach the end posture of punching forward, the end posture is called Ding Shi. We have no power once it is released. We are empty out of power. We have to get into a preparation posture to store or harness the power again. Therefore, the storing power process is filling to full and releasing power process is emptying to null.

When we are in preparation or storing a power, we may be slow as if drawing a bow. However, when we release a power, we have to do it fast and suddenly as if shooting an arrow.

When we use one hand to contact and guide the opponent's power away from our vital area, it is called emptying out, neutralizing or absorbing the opponent's power. At the same time, our other hand is in preparation to punch forward. The empty hand is to defend and neutralize, while the filling to full hand is attacking. When both hands reach the end posture, we switch roles for both hands.

Review:

1. Is the punching hand the full (power) hand?
2. Is the pulling back hand the empty (power) hand?
3. What does it mean to store or harness the power?
4. If you pull the opponent to fall to your rear, then the pulling hand is actually the full (power) hand?
5. What is a stop point of a power in the body?
6. What is a release of a power?
7. What does it mean to empty out the opponent's power?

Chapter 4

Flow

Understanding the flow:

When we step on the ground, we move our foot away and off the ground first. Energy is stored at this higher position. When we land our foot, the stored energy is then released. At the contact point which is the foot, a counter or stopping energy from the ground is received. Most of the energy is absorbed by the joints throughout the body. If we may relay the energy and transfer it via a contact point to the opponent. This is the flow of energy from the ground via us and on to the opponent.

The Qi theory:

It is important to identify the source and the flow of energy of a power produced in each move and posture. The theory of Qi or energy is that the energy may travel from the Dan Tian via pathways toward distal limbs and back. If we consider that our body is a ball or planet, and Dan Tian is the center of gravity or the center of the ball, what the body does is to transfer the energy or a power outward from Dan Tian. When one side of the body receives a power, the energy is centered to Dan Tian and distributed to the rest of the body outward as if expanding or exploding in all directions.

The balance power:

Based on the Dan Tian theory above, when an energy is received or produced by us, it will spread all over the body or distribute outward in all directions. When we do a right punch forward at a punching bag, we may feel energy is traveling to our right foot (if it is the lead foot) to the ground. The front sole of the lead foot has to stop our body from moving forward along with the right fist moving forward. Actually depends on the posture, we may feel energy is going toward all directions to slow and balance our posture so that we do not fall at the end of our moving right fist forward. And the center of direction is Dan Tian.

The resistance power:

When we hit the bag, a counter energy from the bag stopping our right fist is felt and dissipated throughout our body at the moment of the contact.

Analysis of flow of powers in a posture:

When we study and practice each move or posture, we have to understand the source of power, delivery of energy and the balance power. So that we do not fall or injure ourselves. The way to do it right is to practice each move slowly and pay attention to the balance, and the distribution or flow of the energy throughout the body.

In position first:

When we are moving, we are relaxed all over our body. It is easier to move energy or transfer power around. When we start a punch or a low kick, our posture has to be there first before delivery of the energy. This way the power distribution is balanced and reception of counter energy is dissipated in a balance way by the posture in place. For example, if you want to do a right low kick to the right, there will be energy traveling downward toward your left foot at the same time. Your left leg has to be stable or your left knee may absorb some the downward energy and injured. You want to transfer the downward energy all the way to the ground via your supporting leg. You may also lean your upper body leftward a bit, so that you are balance from the left and the right also. And everything is centered on Dan Tian or moving and balancing around it.

The balance game:

Shifting weights between the left and the right side of the body is dependent on putting more weight on the left or the right foot. When we look at the move or posture, we may focus on where is the weight distributed and how it is shifting between the left and the right. We also have to pay attention to balance weight in the front and the rear.

Standing in posture first:

That is why we have to start with standing in posture to align all our body parts the right way or a balance way. After that, we start to practice how to transfer from one posture to another smoothly and slowly. Speed is gained with proficiency over time. The stance and posture practice is called Bai Shi. We have to do this for 6 months or more, before we even think about doing a punch or a kick.

Stepping practice:

The stepping practice is also important. We may solve a lot of fighting problems just by stepping away from the harm coming toward us. How to move with steps in a balance and even way is the lesson that would save your life and get you out of the troubles.

Review:

1. Is the source of energy of a power from the ground?
2. Does the energy of a power start and end with the foot?
3. If we move up our leg, is there an energy stored to be released?
4. How does the energy of a power flow or travel throughout the body?
5. Why that is the energy will be centered on Dan Tian no matter where it starts from the rest of the body?
6. What is the theory of Qi?
7. When we try to deliver energy to one part of the body, is there energy going toward the rest of the body from Dan Tian at the same time to balance our posture relative to the ground due to gravity?
8. How do we receive a counter energy when we hit something with our body part or limb?
9. Do we have to be in the right posture before we punch or kick?
10. What is Bai Shi?
11. Why is practicing stepping method very important?

Chapter 5

Understanding the Opponent's Power

How do we know where the power of the opponent is coming?

At first, we look at his posture and positioning relative to our position. If the opponent's lead hand or lead foot is his right side, he may approach us by advancing his left side. He may also move his lead hand and lead foot forward and the left side follows along.

Secondly, we consider the upper (Shang Pan), mid (Zhong Pan) and lower levels (Xia Pan) of the body.

Finally, we consider our hands to be inside or outside the opponent's arm. The fighting tactics and strategy would be different.

How to contact:

We may use our forearm to contact the opponent's forearm. We have to position ourself relative the opponent in a cross way first. This way we would avoid most of the power the opponent is directing at our previous position.

We may use Tiao to contact the hand coming toward our upper level (head, neck and upper chest). We may use Lan or Gua or mid and low level encounters.

How to listen:

We use a small lateral force to listen or test the opponent's power from the contact point in the wrist or forearm.

Position is everything:

By positioning, we deal with most of the opponent's power from getting to us. We use a small lateral force or circular force to contact and guide his power away from us. We also focus our counter attack with the other side of our body.

The reader may refer to Part I of the Volume 1 of the book for more discussion and review.

Review:

1. What are the 3 factors to consider that where the opponent's power is coming toward us?
2. Are the distance and the opponent's posture the first considering factor?
3. Do we have a strategy to defend the 3 levels of the body?
4. If not, we may always move back or to the side, when the opponent is coming?
5. Why do we have to consider that our defending hands are inside or outside the opponent's arm?
6. How do we position ourself before contacting the opponent?
7. Can we use Tiao to contact the opponent's forearm coming at high?
8. Can we use Lan or Gua for mid and low levels of contact?
9. Do we use a small lateral force to test the direction of the opponent's power?
10. Is our contacting hand the empty hand?
11. Is our counter attacking hand the real or full (power) hand?

Chapter 6

Interaction

There are 4 conducive ways of interaction with the opponent's power.

1. Sticking (Nian):

Once we contact the opponent's forearm, we like to adhere or stick to his forearm. If our elbow is bent and we position to be able to rotate our waist, it is called we are on our front side (Wo Sun). The opponent's elbow is extended and not able to extend any further without bending first, it is called the opponent is on his back side (Ren Bei). If the opponent punches toward us, we move to the side and face his forearm. The positioning gives us the advantage to move further while the opponent is near his full extension of his arm.

2. Following (Shui):

We follow the opponent's hand moves and stepping. If the opponent moves his arm backward, downward, or laterally we follow it without losing contact. We may do a vertical or horizontal circle to follow his arm movement. This way the opponent may not use his hand to approach our vital area. If the opponent moves back a step, we follow by advancing a step and vice versa.

3. Guiding (Dai):

We direct or guide the opponent's power or arm movements. If we are able to follow the opponent's arm movement and steps, we then are able to direct or guide his power further and make him fall to his front or back. We use a lateral force (from rotation of the forearm and the waist) to join or merge into his power by positioning and following the main direction of his power. We also introduce a lateral force to his linear force from rotation of our waist. The opponent's direction of the power is changed or lost by our small lateral force and we are guiding his power to a new direction.

4. Emptying (Kong):

The opponent feels his power is leaving him or being emptying out by the new direction. He is also nearing his full extension of the arm or the end of his power.

For more information and review on the 4 interactions of your power and that of the opponent, please refer to "Tai Ji Quan: theory, practice and fighting methods". There are more discussions with fighting examples in that book.

Review:

1. What is the meaning of sticking to the opponent's power?
2. What does it mean that we are on our front side?
3. What does it mean that we are on our back side?
4. Is the position crossly to the opponent giving us the room for moving forearms and rotation of the waist?
5. How do we follow the opponent's move and power?
6. Does guiding mean that we follow the opponent's move and power and guide it further down the same direction?
7. How do you empty out the opponent's power?
8. Is the stepping or positioning everything in your interaction with the opponent's power?
9. What are the four basic interactions with the opponent's power?

Part II

Characteristic Power

In Part I, we know that we may characterize the nature of a power by its traveling direction (Chapter 1). We know that the source of the power is from the ground. Dan Tian is the center of the body where a power is focused and dissipated outward in all directions (Chapter 2). The concept of emptiness and fullness is useful for referring a power according to its location in the body and time of progression (Chapter 3). The flow of a power is always from Dan Tian exploding outward (Chapter 4). When a power is expressing toward one part of the body, we also issue a power toward the rest of the body to balance our posture without falling. We know about the opponent's power by his position, hand moves and steps (Chapter 5). We may also contact with the opponent's forearm and use a lateral force to listen or test the direction of his power. There are 4 useful ways of interaction with the opponent's power (Chapter 6).

In Part II, some characteristic powers from 5 styles are discussed as examples. The styles are Xing Yi (Chapter 7), Tai Chi (Chapter 8), Ba Gua (Chapter 9), Ba Ji (Chapter 10) and Tong Bei (Chapter 11). The main tactics and strategy of each style with the use of signature powers are also discussed.

Chapter 7

Xing Yi

There are 5 element fist methods in Xing Yi Quan or Form Mind boxing. The posture used is called San Ti Shi. The main power comes from the whole body moving forward or laterally.

1. Splitting (Pi)

Pi is a downward movement of the arm or fist as if using an axe to chop and split a piece of wood. You may also open your palm and use the root of the palm or the whole open palm to Pi the opponent's head, face, nose etc. You move your fist close to your chest. You then open your palm and extend it forward and downward. There is a rotation of the forearm inward. The expression of the power is in the center of the palm. The palm is as high as the nose. The elbow is slightly bent.

2. Thrusting (Beng)

Beng is to advance your fist and steps at the same time. We may practice with both hands pulling back toward the waist and then close the fists and punch forward. The fist starts from the umbilical area. The forearm rotates inward while the fist is advancing. The power is expressed on the face of the fist. The fist form is a vertical fist. Beng Quan is like a shooting arrow.

3. Drilling (Zuan)

Zuan is drilling your fist upward. The spiraling of the forearm may be used to deflect attacks toward your high level. You move the fist close to your chest. You then move your fist forward and upward. You also rotate the forearm outward. Zuan Quan is fast like a discharge of electricity.

4. Canon (Pao)

Pao is to use both arms at the same time as if a canon exploding in all directions. Your left forearm may be rotated inward to deflect attacks while your right fist is punching forward. The Canon fist is explosive.

5. Horizontal (Heng)

Heng is to move the forearm crossly and laterally in a curve. Your arm would move from under the other arm and outward. The shape or form of a Heng fist is a circle and solid. It harmonizes the other 4 fists. The stepping is like that of an S in Heng Quan.

Rotation of the forearm:

We have to pay attention to the rotation of the forearm inward or outward, when we do the five fists. When we pull the fist back, there is also rotation of the forearm. The rotation would increase the power delivered and also serves as a defensive mechanism to deflect the opponent's blocking arm.

The basic 5 fist methods cover all the directions in front of our body. They include the forward movement (Beng), upward movement (Zuan), downward movement (Pi), both lateral and forward movement (Pao), and lateral movement (Heng).

Review:

1. What is the name of the Xing Yi posture?
2. Where is the power coming from in Xing Yi boxing?
3. Is a Pi a downward movement?
4. What is the direction of the power in Beng Quan?
5. What is the direction of the power in Zuan Quan?
6. What are the directions of the power in the Canon fist?
7. What is the traveling path of the power in Heng Quan?
8. Which fist method harmonizes the other 4 fist methods?
9. What is the purpose and function of the rotation of the forearm when we advance the 5 fists?
10. What is the stepping method like in Heng Quan?

Chapter 8

Tai Chi

There are 8 power methods in Tai Chi Quan or grand ultimate boxing. Since Tai Chi moves are circular around joints, there are always components of multiple directions. The spiraling movement of the forearm plus the rotation of the waist are likened to that of a silkworm weaving the silk or Chan Si. In contrast, Pi, Beng, Zhuan and Heng powers of Xing Yi are unidirectional.

1. Extending outward (Peng)

Peng is to move or rotate your forearm outward. You may also move your other body part, such as the shoulder or back outward. It is also called Peng. The main Peng power is from rotation of your waist. It introduces the main laterally outward Peng power in your movement. All the Tai Chi moves contain some form of Peng outward power. The center is Dan Tian. When you shift weight more on the right side of your body, it is the full side and the left side is the empty side.

Peng can be categorized further as upward and outward (Shang Peng), laterally outward (left or right Peng), downward and outward (Lu) etc.

2. Following (Lu)

Lu is used to describe a power from pulling the opponent's forearm or legs laterally or downward and toward your left or right rear. Since you move to the side first, and you are facing the opponent's forearm, you have the room to rotate your waist to the left or right which was your previous rear.

If you pull the opponent's arm with both hands laterally and toward your rear, it is a combination of Peng outward and Lu toward your left or right rear. For the most part, you follow the general direction of the opponent's power. So a Lu power is very light. The main power is again from rotation of the waist.

3. Pushing (Ji)

Ji is to use the hand or forearm to push forward and laterally as if drawing a horizontal circle. If the opponent is Peng moving upward his forearm, you Lu pull his arm laterally and toward your left or right rear with both hands. If the opponent Lu pulls your arm, you move up your steps to be close and Ji push his hands with your forearm or Ji push his open chest with your forearm.

4. Pressing (An)

An is to use your palms to push downward and forward as if drawing a vertical circle. When the opponent is following your Lu power and Ji pushes you. You quickly sit your wrists and push his Ji forearm downward and forward. Ji pushing forward power is now going downward by An from your palms.

Only 4 main characteristic powers are discussed in this chapter. Please refer to "Tai Ji Quan: theory, practice and fighting methods" and the volume 1 of "The treasure book of Chinese martial arts" for more discussion of the other 4 powers.

Review:

1. What is a Peng power?
2. What is a Lu power?
3. What is a Ji power?
4. What is an An power?
5. Does a Peng Jin exist in all Tai Chi moves?
6. Can both Peng and Lu exist in the same move?
7. Where is a Peng Jin expressed from?
8. Does Lu Jin express from a palm?
9. Where is the center of Peng Jin?
10. Does the rotation of the waist provide the main drive for Peng and Lu?
11. Actually, the rotation of the waist drives all 4 characteristic powers?
12. If the opponent Peng pushes you, you Lu pull his forearm?

13. If the opponent Ji pushes you, you quickly sit your palms and An push his forearm?
14. Is sitting the wrist the reason why you may turn the opponent's Ji forward power into An downward power?
15. The palm may absorb the direction of a Ji power and turn it into another direction?

Chapter 9

Ba Gua

Walking power (Zhou Jin)

Some of the basic palm methods in Ba Gua Zhang are discussed in this chapter. Most of the power comes from stepping or walking into a better position. Avoidance of the front with stepping to the side is the main defense theory.

Four types:

There are 4 major types of power in Ba Gua Zhang. They are twisting (Ning), rotating (Gun), horizontal (Heng) and spiraling (Luo Xuan). These powers may happen at the levels of the steps, waist and rotation of the forearm. Thus there are many changes or variations in the fighting methods.

Some specific powers followed:

1. Piercing (Chuan)

The fingers are pointing forward. The palm side may face the left, right, upward or downward. The forearm has upward or Tiao power. Depending on the distance with the opponent, Chuan Zhang may be used to contact the opponent's wrist, forearm and above the elbow. The power is going forward and upward. The power may also go downward and forward along your leg in a half squatting stance.

2. Cloud (Yun)

If the opponent lifts up your elbow joint, you rotate your palm around the elbow joint horizontally to hit the opponent's neck. The palm side is facing upward. If it is blocked by the opponent, we may then flip the palm side and rotate the other way around. It is commonly used in Cheng style. The power travels in a horizontal circle. The power is expressed from the pinkie side.

3. Peeling (Xiao)

You use one hand to hook down the opponent's arm, and use the other hand with palm side down to hit the opponent's neck from the side. This is a common method in Yin style. The power travels in a vertical circle. The power is expressed on the pinkie side.

4. Pushing (Tui)

We push the root of the palm forward. It is also called collapsing palm or Ta Zhang. The power goes forward and downward on the opponent's abdomen.

5. Hitting (Zhuang)

We push forward with open palms. The power is expressed in the center of the palm. If the 2 wrists are close together, it is called "double hitting palm" or Shuang Zhuang Zhang. If they are the shoulder level, it is also called "carrying the moon around your chest" or Huai Zhong Bao Yue. This is a very common palm method in all style.

6. Intercepting (Jie)

When the opponent is hitting your face, you use the side of the palm to intercept. You then quickly attack his face with the other side of the palm. We may also intercept the opponent's hand or leg coming toward our lower level of the body. We do not block the opponent's power abruptly. We follow the general direction of his power for the most part.

7. Guiding (Dai)

We may use the piercing palm to contact the opponent's wrist and forearm. We then use a downward or lateral force to pull and guide his power further and make him fall to his front. This is a common Qin Na and throw technique. We have to step to the side or back first. The power is expressed from your grabbing or hooking fingers. The main power comes from your body lowering or moving with rotation of the waist.

8. Leading (Lin)

We follow the direction of the opponent's power and lead it further. The opponent's power is emptied out. Our power comes from stepping or walking along the same direction of the opponent's power.

9. Entangling (Chan)

We circle around our wrist to control the opponent's wrist and forearm. This is a common restraining method. The power comes from the wrist and rotation of the forearm.

10. Hooking (Diao)

Use the thumb and the index finger to hook the opponent's wrist. The power is expressed from the fingers. The main power is the whole body movement to move the opponent's arm to the left, right, crossly upward or crossly downward.

11. Sticking (Zhan)

Once we contact the opponent's forearm, we follow his movement and remain in contact.

12. Testing (Tang)

Four fingers closed together are pointing forward and upward. It is used to hit the chest, face, or rib side. It is commonly used in Yin style. The power is expressed with finger tips.

13. Opening and closing (Kai He)

When we move our forearm outward laterally, it is called opening palm. If the 2 arms are coming together, it is called closing palm. For example, with 2 wrists close together and palm side upward, it is called "white ape presenting the peach". It is a closing palm. The power comes from the forearm coming together or separating.

14. Axe (Pi)

You move your palm downward to strike. The power is expressed from the forearm and the palm. We have to have a whole body sinking downward power, too.

15. Lifting (Tuo)

Use your palm to lift up the opponent's elbow. It is a defensive move. The power is expressed in the center of the palm. We may use both hands in turn to lift. It is also called "a butterfly flying among the flower" or Hu Die Chuan Hua. We may also lift both palms at the same time and use the forearms to deflect the opponent's forearm. It is called "great eagle spreading wing" or Da Peng Zhan Chi.

16. Rib side hitting (Ye)

Use the palm to hit downward on the abdomen or rib side. The power goes downward.

17. Spiraling (Luo Xuan)

The power comes from the rotation of the forearm. It is a small power but every effective. It is one of the four characteristic powers in Ba Gua Zhang. It exists in many palm methods, such as piercing, testing, opening, closing and entangling palms.

18. Absorbing (Xi Hua)

The power comes from the rotation of the waist. If we are restrained by the opponent, we may rotate our waist to the left or right. The restrain is broken off by absorption to the left or the right.

19. Rotating (Gun)

The rotation of the forearm may be used to deflect the opponent's attacking arm. Our elbow is also close to the opponent's now open chest or rib side. We may use the elbow to strike his open soft spots.

For more information on Ba Gua Zhang, please refer to "Ba Gua Zhang: techniques and application" and volume 1 of "The treasure book of Chinese martial arts".

Review:

1. What are the 4 major characteristic powers in Ba Gua Zhang?
2. Is the main power from the stepping to the side in Ba Gua Zhang?
3. Why that is there are many changes or variations in the fighting methods of Ba Gua Zhang?
4. Why is the penetrating palm the common defensive method in the style?
5. What is a cloud palm?
6. What to do if the opponent blocks your cloud palm?
7. What is a peeling palm?
8. What are the directions of the power from a pushing palm?
9. What is a Ta Zhang?
10. Is the hitting palm common among all styles of Ba Gua Zhang?
11. Do you use a lot of power in an intercepting palm?
12. What is the general direction of an intercepting palm?
13. Is a guiding palm a common way of throw?
14. Where is the power coming from in a leading palm?
15. Is an entangling palm method a common way to restrain the opponent?
16. How do you hook the opponent's wrist?
17. How do you stick to the opponent's forearm?
18. Is a testing palm commonly used in Yin style?
19. What is an opening palm method?
20. What is a closing palm method?
21. What is the direction of the power in an axe palm?
22. Is Tuo Zhang a defensive move?
23. What is the direction of a Ye Zhang?
24. Where is the power coming from in the spiraling palm method?
25. How do you absorb the opponent's restraining power?
26. What is a Gun Zhang?

Chapter 10

Ba Ji

Open the door:

There are 6 major characteristic powers in Ba Ji fist. The main tactics and strategy of the style is to open the door forcibly and close in on to the opponent at the same time. The closer you are to the opponent, more powerful Ba Ji moves will be.

1. Sinking (Xia Cheng or Cheng Zhui)

The whole body moves downward by bending the knees and sitting on the hip. The elbow and fist moves downward at the same time. This is the most important power in Ba Ji fist. The focus is on Dan Tian. The stepping method is very heavy as if a bull is lying down.

2. Thrusting (Chong)

If you stamp on your foot and move the other foot forward, there is a power coming from the whole body thrusting forward. This is called Chuang Bu. Your punching fist carries more power from the whole body accelerating forward. You may use the same stepping method for the elbow and knee strikes, and the shoulder and hip strikes (Kao).

3. Extending (Cheng)

The power comes from Dan Tian and moves outward in all directions. If you extend your fist upward and forward, it is called Cheng Chui. The elbow and the knee, the shoulder and the hip, and the fist and the foot have to be in harmony or unison, so that the body is balance in extending the power outward. We may use our fist to punch and the foot to kick at the same time.

We may also use the elbow and the knee to strike at the same time. We may use the shoulder and the hip to hit at the same time. This is how we may attack at high, mid and low level at the same time. (San Pan Lian Ji)

4. Entangling (Chan)

We may circle around the wrist, elbow and the shoulder (Chan Wan, Chan Zhou and Chan Bei) to restrain the opponent's forearm and open his door. This is the common way to enter the opponent's vital area. The power is from the circling around the joints and stepping forward and to the side.

5. Cross (Shi Zhi)

The power comes from the hands or forearms coming close together and then separating. They are crossing or circular movements from the left to the right (vice versa) and then going forward and backward. The movement of 2 hands or 2 forearms looks like a cross. Thus the name is a cross. It may be used to restrain or throw the opponent. We apply powers going toward opposing directions at the same time. From bending the arm around the elbow joint, the head around the neck joint, the body around the waist joint, the upper body and the leg around the hip joint etc, we may restrain and throw the opponent. It is also called "tying up the godly rope" or Kun Xian Shen.

6. Inch (Cun)

We may have a big movement of the whole body. However, we deliver the power only within an inch away from the target area. We may also use the inch power to intercept and restrain the opponent's forearm. It is called Cun Jie Cun Na. The inch power has a short distance to travel. We use the whole body weight moving or sinking to drive the move.

For more information, please refer to "Ba Zi Jie Xi: a talk on rake fist" and volume 1 of the book.

Review:

1. Is the Xia Cheng Jin the most important power in Ba Ji?
2. How do you develop the sinking power?
3. What is a thrusting power?

4. How do you do a Chuang Bu?
5. How do you develop an extending power?
6. What is a Cheng Chui?
7. Is the entangling power or Chan Si used commonly to restrain the opponent's arm and open his door?
8. What is a cross power?
9. How do you express an inch power?
10. Is the cross power used to restrain and throw the opponent?

Chapter 11

Tong Bei

Going long:

There are 5 element palm methods in Tong Bei Quan or extended back boxing. They are equivalent to metal, wood, water, fire and earth. The tactics and strategy of the style is to go long and extend far.

Extending power

The back is arched. We extend the back, the shoulder and the arm, when we point and strike. We then bend our wrist, elbow and back again. The posture is like that of an ape. When we start to strike, we may move forward and upward. However, when we strike, we sit on the hip and there is an downward power.

Three points aligned:

The ape like posture protects our vital area by shrinking the abdomen, one elbow protecting the rib side, and one hand near the lead hand elbow. The nose, the hand and the lead foot are always on a line in both the ready and strike postures. The 3 points aligned is called San Jian Xiang Zhao. This way our vital area is shielded.

1. Throwing palm (Shuai Zhang, metal)

You move your palm close to your midline. You then use the back side of the hand to hit forward on the upper level of the opponent. We have to shake or vibrate the wrist joint to express the power.

Harnessing power (Xu Jin)

The power comes from the foot and travels all the way to the hand. We have to relax our body overall. When we stand on the front sole (Deng), there is a counter energy produced from the ground. We then transfer this energy all the way to the hand. We may bend the knee and arch our back with a bent elbow. This is the preparation or harnessing the power posture.

Releasing power (Fa Jin)

We suddenly land our heels (Ta) and extend the hand outward. The landing of the heels and the back hand striking downward happen at the same time. We have to sit on our hip. We may also advance our lead foot and the rear foot follows. Our other hand has to have a power pulling backward while the throwing palm is extending forward.

2. Tapping palm (Pai Zhang, wood)

You pull your hand back and then extend the palm forward and tap with the palm side down. You express your power from the center of palm to hit the opponent's face, nose etc. The requirement of the body method is the same as in throwing palm.

3. Penetrating palm (Chuan Zhang, water)

You circle your palm and pull back as if grabbing the opponent's forearm and pulling it downward. You then extend your arm and "stab" forward your vertical palm. You also move up your steps. The power is expressed at the fingertips. You are hitting focused soft point such as the throat. The body method is the same as above.

4. Axe palm (Pi Zhang, fire)

You swing your whole arm upward and then downward as if drawing a big circle around your shoulder joint. The power is expressed from the back and waist.

5. Drilling palm (Zuan Zhang, earth)

You use one hand penetrating forward and upward. You then pull the hand back. At the same time, you move your other fist forward. The knuckle of the middle finger is protruding. The power is expressed at the protruding knuckle. It is to hit a focused soft spot at the chest and abdomen.

Opening the door:

When we move the attacking hand back, we may grab and pull the opponent's blocking forearm. In Pi Zhang, we move to the side of the opponent, push down his arm and open his door.

For more information, please refer to volume I of the book.

Review:

1. Is the power generated from the foot in Tong Bei?
2. What is Deng?
3. What is Ta?
4. How do you do a throwing palm?
5. Does the throwing palm express the power from a shaking wrist?
6. Is the center of the palm the power expressed from a tapping palm?
7. Is the fingertip the power expressed from a penetrating palm?
8. In a drilling palm, the power is expressed from the knuckle of the middle finger?
9. Is Pi Zhang used to open the opponent's door?
10. When we move back our attacking hand, we may use it to pull the opponent's blocking arm?

Part III

Development of Power

In Part II, some characteristic powers from 5 styles are studied. We may see each style has its own unique way of generating and using power. In other words, they focus on different ways of power generating to solve fighting problems. However, there are also some common and overlapping methods, too.

In Part III, some general ways of training and developing power are discussed. Each style has its own way of training for the specific power it needs.

Chapter 12

Relaxation Exercise

The Purpose:

We have to relax the joints, tendon and muscle before engaging more vigorous physical activity. We warm up our body. After some static stance in our daily life, our muscle is "cold".

Each style has specific drills for relaxation purpose and strengthening the joints and muscle over time.

How to practice:

1. We rotate around the wrist, elbow, shoulder, waist, hip, knee and ankle clockwise and counterclockwise for 8 times. This way all of our joints are loosen up.
2. We slowly punch forward and grab and pull back the arm. We then swing down the fist to the front and to the side.
3. We do low kick to the front, to the side and to the back several times. In short, we have a small and slow version of the range of motions that we are about to do in full scale.

Review:

1. Why do we have to do some moderate exercise before we practice?
2. How do we loosen the joints?
3. How do we loosen the muscle and tendon?
4. What does it mean that our muscle is cold?

Chapter 13

Standing Practice

The Purpose:

Each style has its own specific stances and postures. Usually, we have to practice to stand in these stances and postures for from a few minutes to 25 minutes. We train our body to remember the right posture. The standing practice will also train our endurance. Once we are aware of these postures. It would be easier for us to detect the changes from these postures.

How to practice:

We have to relax our body. We may feel and sense the distribution and balance of power within our body. Again we focus our attention to Dian Tian. We then focus to different body parts and limbs. We clear our thoughts, emotions and memories. Just have a clear and focused mind to sense the power and Qi from the environment and throughout our body. We may start to stand for a few minutes. We may stand longer in postures over time. The longer we stand, more static and tensile strength we may develop for our muscle, tendon, bone and joints.

Relaxation exercise:

After standing for some time, we have to loosen up the muscle by hitting them gently. We may use fists to hit the thighs. We may use the foot to hit the back of the other leg etc. We may also do some stretching.

General requirements:

Requirements for each posture are different in each style. In general, 10 toes grabbing on to the ground, sitting on the hip, focusing on Dan Tian, shoulders relaxed and dropped, the elbows sinking etc.

Some examples:

A. Liang Yi Zhuang (Ba Ji)

The Liang Yi horse stance practice from Ba Ji style. The head should have a pushing upward power or Ding Jin, as if supporting the blue sky. The feet are like stepping into a clear stream. The chest should be tugged in as if carrying a baby. The elbows are pushing outward as if pushing against mountains. The pushing power or Ding Jin is the main power in the posture of Ba Ji fist. There is a circle within the square structure of the posture.

B. Bear stance (Ba Gua)

The pressing palms are close to the thighs. The shoulder has to be dropped. The back has to be relaxed and slightly arched. The chest is tugged in. The elbows are slightly bent. The knees are tugged in in the horse stance. There is the extending outward power in the center of the palm and the whole body. Your whole body structure is aligned to express the extending power or Cheng Jin. And it is also a circular power or Yuan Cheng Jin. The extending and circular power is the main power in the posture of Ba Gua Zhang.

C. Tai Chi (Tai Chi)

The neck is loose as if suspended. The Qi is focused on the Bai Hui Xue on top of the skull. The shoulders are dropped. The chest is slightly tugged in. The elbows are sinking. We bring the palms close together in the front at the shoulder level. Our arms form a circle. We focus on Dan Tian. We feel the Qi flow along meridians in the midline of the body both in the front and the back. This is the small circuit from Bai Hui Xue to Hui Yin Xue in the middle of the groin area. We may also feel the Qi flow to the fingers and back and to the toes and back. We place our tongue against the palate. We relax all over our body. The main thing is that we focus and center our Qi or power flow in the midline of the body. Overtime, we are aware of the center line. When we rotate our waist along the line, we may produce the Peng Jin laterally. This is the main power in Tai Chi. Our body structure is relaxed and is able to extend or Peng outward, too. The center of Qi flow and power production is in Dan Tian. Everything goes outward from there.

Review:

1. Why do we practice standing in postures?
2. How long do we have to practice in each session?
3. Do we have to relax our body while in standing?
4. What kind of a mindset we should have in standing?
5. Do we have the results from standing practice right away or overtime?
6. What do we do after standing in posture for a while?
7. What are general requirements for a standing practice?
8. How do you do Liang Yi Zhuang in Ba Ji style?
9. What is the main power in Liang Yi posture?
10. How do you do a bear stance in Ba Gua?
11. Is Yuan Cheng Jin the main power in Ba Gua?
12. How do you do a Tai Chi posture?
13. Is Peng Jin the main power in Tai Chi?

Chapter 14

Equipment Training

The Purpose:

There are many training equipments to help us to practice, such as a punching bag, a punching pad, wooden dummies and other type of dummies etc. We may practice actual power generation and expression. We may also have some feedback experiences from the punching bag or pad.

Safety:

We always want to do a slow or gradual training session. We start with practice to be accurate in hitting with our posture in the right and balance way. We start to hit harder and harder over time. Always consult a teacher with a training session. If we are not careful, we may seriously injure ourself. Wear the necessary protective gears, too.

Examples:

1. A flour or sand bag:

We may practice our hand's grabbing power by tossing the 1# flour bag in the air and then grab it with other hand. We may increase the weight up to 5# over time.

2. A bundle of chopsticks:

We try to grab and twist in the opposing direction with both hands at the same time. This is to practice twisting power.

3. A rope:

We circle our wrist and grab the rope. This is to practice the entanglement power or Chan Si Jin.

4. A staff:

We may practice to circle and grab the staff. We may practice Tiao, Lan and Gua, too. The staff is like the forearm or the leg of the opponent.

5. A piece of cloth or paper:

We may hang pieces of cloth or paper in high, mid and low levels. We may practice target hitting and kicking. The purpose is to be accurate and fast in timing. No hard hitting is necessary.

6. A pot of beans or sand:

We may practice our finger stabbing power.

7. Some weights:

We may practice our lifting power or upward pushing power by lifting some weights. We start with one pound and gradually increase to 25 #. We may also tie the weights to our wrist or ankle and practice moves slowly. Overtime, when we remove the weights, our hands and legs will be faster and more powerful.

8. A punching bag:

We may practice a lot of things with the bag. We may punch and kick. We may do elbow and knee strike. We may do shoulder and hip strike. We may do chest and back strike. We may push with open palm etc. It is very good to practice to hit a wider area. It is not good for practice of focused point strike such as finger stabbing. The resistance is too hard and wide. We would injure our fingers easily.

9. A dummy:

There are many types of dummy. Each has its purpose of training. The common wooden dummy is with 2 upper poles, a low pole (simulating the forearm) and a leg pole. We may practice a lot of common moves with it.

10. A standing pole:

We may cover the pole with cushion and practice hitting high and low from the side. We may walk around it as in Ba Gua Zhang to practice walking in a circle. We may also place several poles arranged in a certain way. We practice hitting them as if they are multiple opponents.

There is more equipment for training. We only discussed 10 examples in this chapter.

Review:

1. Is the flour bag good for practicing the grabbing power?
2. Is a bundle of chopsticks good for training the twisting power?
3. Is a rope good for training Chan Si Jin?
4. Can we practice Tiao, Lan and Gua with a staff?
5. Is a piece of a cloth good for target hitting practice?
6. Is a pot of beans good for practicing finger stabbing power?
7. What kind of power may be practiced with weights?
8. Name 3 things that we may practice with a punching bag.
9. Name one thing that we may not practice with a punching bag.
10. What is a common dummy?
11. Name 2 things we may practice with a standing pole.

Chapter 15

Partner Training

The Purpose:

We may learn almost all the lessons from our training partner. We may work out and learn a technique with a cooperative partner. We may also spar with a resistant partner. A good training partner may teach us a lot.

Safety:

We always have to be aware of the danger involved in a technique. We want to learn. We also do not want to injure our teacher which is the training partner. A good mattress and some safety measures in place are necessary in a studio. A guiding teacher is always a good thing, too.

Examples:

There are 2 man drill sets. We may take turns to practice each part with a partner. There are also push hand exercises. Each style has its own one man drill and 2 man drill practice sets.

There is an old saying. "We are only as good as our training partner". It means that we can only learn well from a good training partner. It is very important to practice with a good partner. Everything we practice will come alive with the training partner.

Review:

1. Can we work out a technique with a cooperative training partner?
2. Can we spar with a resistant partner?

3. Do we have to be aware of the danger involved in a technique when we practice with a partner?
4. A good mattress and safe ways to fall would keep us from injury?
5. Why do we practice 2 man drill set?
6. Why do we practice push hand exercise?

Concluding Remark

This volume is a continuation from the volume 1. This book gives the reader a basic idea about consideration of power generation, balance and transfer. It is very important to know about the power factors. This is why and how we do moves the way we do. If we do not pay attention to the power distribution and balance, our moves lose their purpose. And our practice is useless. Finally, Chinese martial arts training have 3 tiers. The first tier is to practice all the moves alone. The second tier is to practice with equipments. The third tier would be to practice with a partner. If we are in a hurry or just not doing the first 2 tiers, and jump to the third. We may have to go back to tier 1 and 2. These 3 tiers are all necessary meaning we do them all and not just one without the other 2. It would be nice from lesson 1 on day 1, you spar. But without proper basic training, you would pick up a lot of bad habits. And these bad habits will be very difficult to correct later on. On the other hand, if a school only provides the first 2 tiers and does not offer sparring. Then everything seems to be hanging in the air. We would never appreciate the training if we never use them to spar. Have a happy and safe training with your teacher and fellow students. We will meet again in future books.